REGARDS...

Dominique Amouroux

THE VILLA SAVOYE

ÉDITIONS DU PATRIMOINE
CENTRE DES MONUMENTS NATIONAUX

INTRODUCTION

Designed during a series of brief creative sessions by a prolific pair of young architects, financed by a man indifferent to the desire to possess, wanted by a woman whom its flaws would exasperate, occupied and vandalised, destined for the scrap yard by the French government in charge of passing down knowledge, saved by its architect and his loyal friends with a minister's support, this house is now a miraculously surviving manifesto, a octogenarian that hasn't aged a bit, and a paradoxical joy.
It was at the end of the summer of 1928 that a stylish couple, Pierre and Eugénie Savoye, commissioned two fashionable architects, Le Corbusier and Pierre Jeanneret, to design their weekend house. Completed three years later, "Les Heures Claires" would become, after many ups and downs, one of the most famous houses of 20th-century architecture, known throughout the world as the "Villa Savoye" and attributed solely to Le Corbusier.

A paradoxical commission

Established in Lille—and in partnership with Gustave Gras from 1907—Pierre Savoye quickly made a substantial fortune as the director of a company offering insurance contracts to large industrial groups in the textile, mining, and chemicals sectors of northern France. But, profoundly affected by the First World War, he was convinced that a new conflict was inevitable, that exoduses and destruction would result; for these reasons, he refused to purchase any property. He was thus only the tenant of the flat that the family lived in at

Promotion.
Le Corbusier presented the model of the villa at exhibitions in the United States and Europe even after it was built, here in 1935.

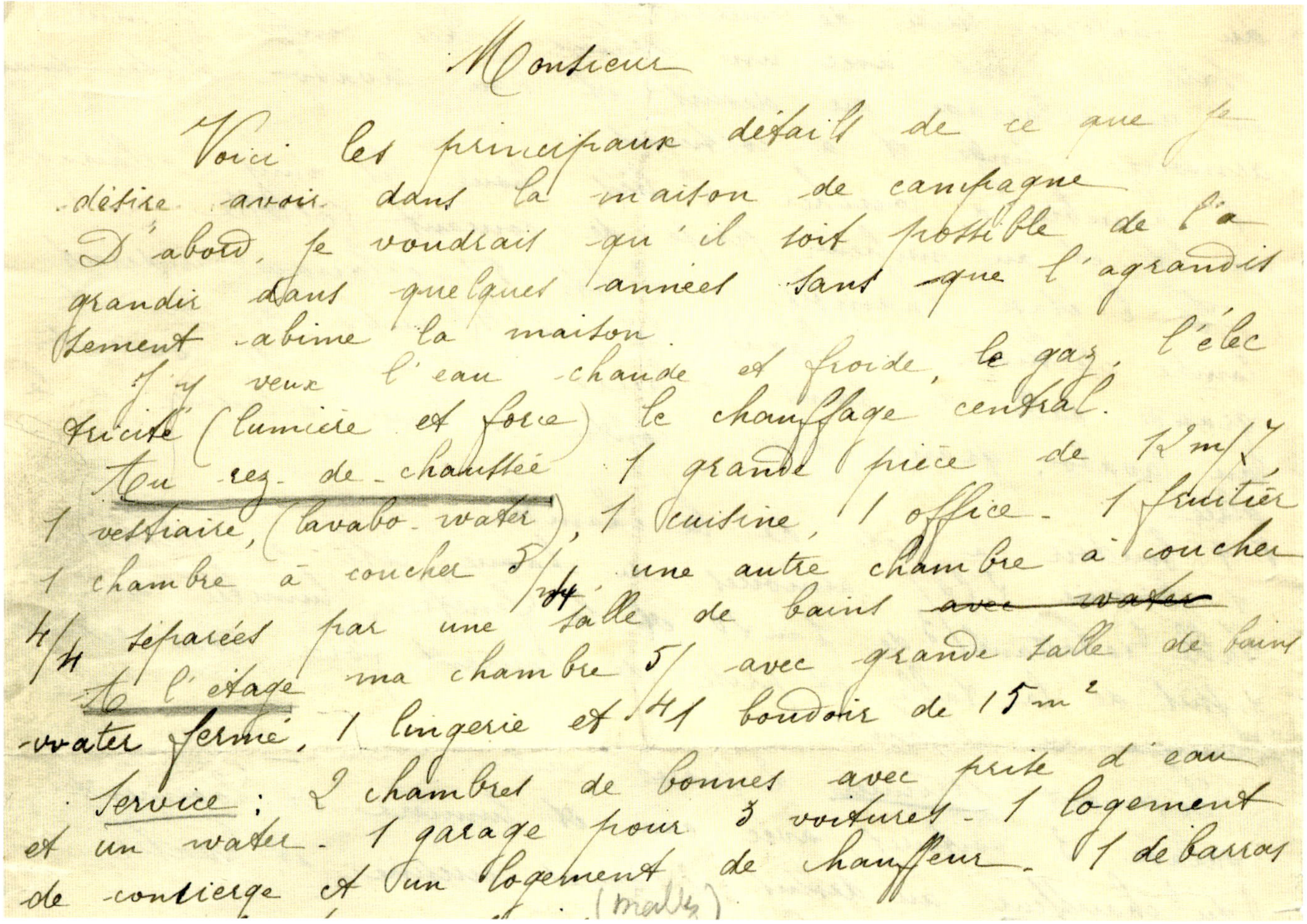

Monsieur

Voici les principaux détails de ce que je désire avoir dans la maison de campagne

D'abord, je voudrais qu'il soit possible de l'agrandir dans quelques années sans que l'agrandissement abime la maison.

J'y veux l'eau chaude et froide, le gaz, l'électricité (lumière et force) le chauffage central.

Au rez-de-chaussée 1 grande pièce de 12m/7 1 vestiaire, (lavabo-water), 1 cuisine, 1 office. 1 fruitier 1 chambre à coucher 5/4, une autre chambre à coucher 4/4 séparées par une salle de bains ~~avec water~~

A l'étage ma chambre 5/ avec grande salle de bains water fermé, 1 lingerie et 1 boudoir de 15m²

Service : 2 chambres de bonnes avec petite [illegible] d'eau et un water. 1 garage pour 3 voitures. 1 logement de concierge et un logement de chauffeur. 1 débarras (malles)

Eugénie Savoye, letter of September 1928: "Here are the principal details of what I would like to have in the country house" (Fondation Le Corbusier, Paris, H1-12-370).

105 rue de Courcelles in the 17th arrondissement of Paris from 1928, the year the Gras Savoye firm opened its first office in the French capital on rue Pierre-Pelouse, on the edge of the 8th arrondissement.

Nevertheless, that same year, Pierre Savoye granted Eugénie's wish for a weekend house. Her husband's attitude explains why she drew up the detailed brief of the future house for the architects, and why numerous estimates and letters sent by the contractors to the designers refer to "Madame Savoye's villa". Pierre Jeanneret and Le Corbusier for the most part communicated with her, her husband only really making an appearance when financial matters were dealt with, notably the extra work to remedy the problems with the house.

To fulfil his wife's wish, Pierre Savoye purchased 7 of the 52 hectares that made up the grounds of the Château de Villiers in Poissy, about 30 kilometres from Paris. His friend Donat Agache, president of the board of directors of Établissements Kuhlmann and director of the Établissements Agache Fils, of the Compagnie des Chemins de Fer du Nord, and of the Compagnie des Mines d'Anzin, had just bought this huge piece of land. Agache reserved the existing chateau for the leisure activities of the company employees, but personally took possession of 25 hectares on which he had a Neo-Norman residence built in 1928. On the same parcelled-out property there were soon three residences that still assert their own style today: the Château de Villiers, refurbished by the architect Théophile Bourgeois; the Agache house, designed by the architect Henri Jacquelin; and the Villa Savoye, designed by Jeanneret and Le Corbusier.

A sporting location

In addition to the friendly surroundings, Pierre Savoye and his wife could practise their favourite sport on the greens of the recently developed Saint-Germain golf club or those of La Boulie in Versailles, which opened in 1901. The couple was certainly aware of the residential appeal of the western suburbs of Paris. This trend, which began in the previous century with the creation of the development of Le Vésinet, was confirmed in the early decades of the 20th century with the construction of avant-garde residences for famous personalities, such as that built by Robert Mallet-Stevens for the couturier Paul Poiret in Mézy-sur-Seine, about 20 kilometres from Poissy. Le Corbusier himself accompanied this westward expansion of the French capital by building studios and villas for artists in Boulogne-sur-Seine, Vaucresson, Garches, and Ville-d'Avray.

Choosing an architect

The couple, receptive to the creations of its time, contacted Le Corbusier whose fame was already firmly established through his manifesto-works of 1925, such as the Pavillon de l'Esprit Nouveau, built with the context of the Exposition Internationale des Arts Décoratifs in Paris, and the Plan Voisin for the urban renewal of the Right Bank of Paris by means of tall buildings. He was also known for his built works, both public—including the Palais du Peuple for the Salvation Army in Paris—or private, particularly the studios and houses designed in Paris and its suburbs for Amédée Ozenfant, Georges Besnus, Raoul La Roche, Albert Jeanneret, Jacques Lipchitz, Oscar Miestchaninoff, William and Jeanne Cook, Gabrielle de Monzie, and Michael and Sarah Stein, or abroad, such as those of the Weissenhof Estate in Stuttgart, Germany. It was,

Portrait of Pierre Jeanneret (1896–1987). An architect and designer, and the co-author of the manifesto "Cinq points vers une nouvelle architecture" ("Five Points towards a New Architecture"), he played an essential role in the design and construction of the "white villas" and the city of Chandigarh, India.

Le Corbusier, photographed with the model of the Ville Radieuse, a project he was working on while designing the Villa Savoye with Pierre Jeanneret.

moreover, to one of the architect's "white villas"—built in Ville-d'Avray for Henry and Barbara Church, the fabulously wealthy founders of the review *Mesures* with Jean Paulhan—that Eugénie Savoye referred to express her vision of the future kitchen of her house to the architects.

An intense and prolific period

While the Villa Savoye was being designed and built, from 1929 to 1931, Le Corbusier—alone or with Pierre Jeanneret—founded the Congrès Internationaux d'Architecture Moderne (CIAM), whose first conference was held in La Sarraz, Switzerland. He designed the Centrosoyuz (Ministry of Light Industry) in Moscow; designed the Cité Internationale des Connaissances called the Mundaneum, where he laid the foundations for the museum of unlimited growth, for Paul Otlet and Henri La Fontaine; and built the Clarté building in Geneva and the Swiss pavilion of the Cité Universitaire Internationale de Paris. He designed and had work started on the Rue Nungesser-et-Coli building, drew up town-planning proposals for Algiers, and won the competition for the headquarters of the League of Nations in Geneva. He presented furniture designed with Charlotte Perriand, including the renowned LC4 chaise longue, the LC1 sling chair, the LC2 armchair, and the LC6 table, at the Salon d'Automne. He travelled to the Eastern bloc, Latin America, and North Africa. He published *Précisions sur un état présent de l'architecture et de l'urbanisme* (Paris: Crès, 1930) and the first volume of his complete works, in the form of a collection of plates published by Albert Morancé in Paris. This "album", published as *Oeuvres récentes de Le Corbusier et P. Jeanneret* and sold for 100 francs, invited its readers to "be up to date with modern architecture" and "understand what is in fashion today so as not to be put out by what will be in fashion tomorrow".

Yet, none of this intense activity seemed to be reflected in the design and construction of the Villa Savoye. The faults noticed later were more due to the inexperience of the contractor Cormier in the implementation of new processes or the underestimation by the two architects of the weather conditions affecting the hill whipped by the marine winds that no relief, apart from the cliffs of the Pays de Caux, impeded.

Opulent.
When they arrived in Paris in 1928, Pierre and Eugénie Savoye lived in Rue de Courcelles, in a neighbourhood with Haussmannian architecture near the Parc Monceau. Postcard, early 20th century (author's collection).

Similar urban settings

Pierre and Eugénie Savoye met the architects eight years after Charles-Édouard Jeanneret had chosen the pseudonym Le Corbusier and six years after he had started working with his cousin, Pierre. When he was not kept from Paris by his business trips, Le Corbusier divided his time between 35 rue de Sèvres, where his office was located—between the Hôtel Lutétia and the Bon Marché department store in the run-down premises of a congregation of Jesuits—and his accommodation at 20 rue Jacob, which he left in 1931 to move into the flat-atelier of the top floor of the building he had just completed in Rue Nungesser-et-Coli, near the Bois de Boulogne.

Pierre and Eugénie Savoye and their son Roger also lived in a well-to-do neighbourhood, that of the Rue de Courcelles that runs, not far from the Place de l'Étoile, from Parc Monceau to the present Place du Maréchal-Juin.

Although the Savoyes and Le Corbusier lived and worked in classical settings and Haussmannian surroundings, an avant-garde aesthetic universe was forming in Poissy with the active complicity of Pierre Jeanneret.

A simply stated request

The two architects worked from a brief drawn up by Eugénie Savoye who, in a short letter of September 1928, listed the needs of the family and expressed detailed preferences in certain technical details.

She asked that the future house be able to be extended without damage. She wanted modern conveniences: hot and cold water, electricity (light and power), and central heating. On the ground floor, she wanted the reception rooms (the entrance and a fair-sized cloakroom) and living areas (the kitchen, the dining room, and the living room), a bedroom for their son and a guestroom, two maid's rooms, accommodation for the concierge or the gardener, and another room for the chauffeur. Also a garage for three cars, a box room for tools, an attic for trunks, and two cellars including a wine cellar because the house was meant to welcome the couple's family, friends, and acquaintances. She asked for a large bedroom, a bathroom with toilet, a linen room, and a boudoir upstairs.

She specified that the living room did not have to be strictly rectangular and that it should have comfortable corners and a large fireplace. She stipulated that the pantry, "a little larger than that of Ville-d'Avray", should have a space for an electric washing machine, thus marking the appearance of electrical appliances in the interiors of large residences. This openness to technological advances was confirmed by the wish to put a rubber carpet in the bedrooms and insulating material on the exterior walls "to protect the house from heat and cold".

This is how a modern home designed for entertaining and living on a single level, and pleasant moments spent in a house and grounds well-maintained by servants and employees was envisaged. A lot of space was given to the automobile; there were plans for three: that of the husband, who only travelled with his chauffeur; that of Eugénie, who drove; and probably the future car of their son or simply that of guests invited to spend a weekend at a house soon dubbed "Les Heures Claires". Also taking shape in the mind of Eugénie Savoye was a hive of activity on the lower level and a private, serene space reserved for the couple upstairs. Attention was also paid to the financing of the project; her letter ended with a request for a "descriptive, quantitative" estimate from the architects and an agreement that "all work that is more or less than estimated will be added to or deducted from the fixed price".

Cluttered.
From 1917, when he moved to Paris, to 1933, Le Corbusier lived in a classic flat located at 20 rue Jacob, in the heart of the Latin Quarter (Fondation Le Corbusier, Paris).

Lively.
Le Bon Marché, one of the department stores of Paris, attracted crowds to the Rue de Sèvres where Le Corbusier and Pierre Jeanneret's office was located. Postcard, early 20th century (author's collection).

The detailed elements of this commission recall a letter from Le Corbusier to one of his clients, Madame Meyer: "This has matured slowly, caressed on days of perfect calm, opposite a highly classical site. We dreamt of building a house as smooth and plain as a well-proportioned chest, unencumbered by a multitude of features creating a contrived picturesqueness." In fact, while the main idea seemed to have emerged very quickly, it took several successive approaches before the project was finalised.

Five different projects

In a week of work, 6–14 October 1928, Le Corbusier and Pierre Jeanneret disrupted the layout specified by Eugénie Savoye. They took advantage of the configuration of the plot overlooking the Seine valley to evoke the Athenian acropolis. They designed a long drive to bring automobiles into the heart of the building, borrowed North African references to organise the path through the interior space, and put into play elements of their joint theory to give shape to the project. The visual and spatial momentum was given, the square plan established, and the idea of the central ramp hit on, but the first estimations of 5 November were close to 800,000 francs—twice the allocated budget.

The very next day, the architects took the project in an entirely different direction thanks to a drastic reduction in the total surface area of the house. They thus arrived at a cost of 350,000 francs, without finding satisfactory functional solutions. In late November, this double setback led them to rethink the space: they abandoned the curved forms, increased the size of the terraces, and affirmed each function or group of functions as an architecturally autonomous entity in a now rectangular site plan.

"Unencumbered by a multitude of features", this third approach deprived the project of its initial visual clarity: it was abandoned in mid-December for a fourth design that took up the foundations of the first design and laid down the main principles that led to the fifth project, which was adopted Construction began in April 1929. The project was characterised by the automobile traffic gliding under the pilotis, the garage integrated into the habitable volume of the ground floor, the diurnal and nocturnal living areas brought together upstairs, the ramp and the side servants' stairs displayed in the central space, a single roof garden looking out onto the west, the bedrooms placed at right angles on the east and south façades, the dining room and the living room united in a single volume on the north façade, facing the view over the Seine valley.

The whole is contained in a compact plan elaborated using a layout grid of 4.75 x 4.75 metres. The house has a habitable surface area of 440 square metres and a total surface area of 875 square metres, including 110 square metres of roof garden and 250 square metres of terrace, including the 70-square metre solarium.

Many further adjustments were made, including during construction, notably in the layout of the accommodation for the chauffeur and the warden; in the end, the chauffeur had small quarters on the ground floor of the villa, the warden a house built at the entrance of the property.

The role of the automobile

Interestingly, each of the successive projects organised the ground floor of the Villa Savoye around the automobile. It was possible to live in Paris and have a holiday home built in Poissy—even before the Autoroute de l'Ouest, scheduled for 1935 but postponed until 1946, opened—because the automobile was from that point on reliable. Hence its particularly rapid development: while the photographs of the streets of Paris taken in 1900 showed pedestrians, carriages, and omnibuses, those taken in 1930 attest to already dense traffic.

Like the drawings by the two architects, the photographs of architecture emphasised automobiles, their imposing volumes and dark colours, in the foreground of the "white villas" and other spotlessly white Corbusian buildings. Sometimes parked in front of the door of the residence, they penetrated the interior space as was the case, for example, of

the garage of the Villa Stein-de-Monzie in Vaucresson, completed in 1928.

A cinematographic approach

The cinematographic link between architecture and the automobile established by the director Marcel L'Herbier and the architect Robert Mallet-Stevens in the film *L'Inhumaine* (*The Inhuman Woman*), released in December 1924, found a new development in the Villa Savoye.

After having driven past Poissy, the visitor takes the road that goes along a wooded hillside, then leads to a vast plateau of farmland. On his right, in a long stone wall, opens the entrance to the Villa Savoye. As his car turns into it, he is fleetingly brought face to face with the disconcerting image of a small white structure, perched on pilotis, with façades slashed by horizontal windows. Nothing relates this compact volume formally to the classical or eclectic houses that as a rule punctuate the beginning of the straight drive leading to the country residences of the aristocracy or the upper middle classes. There is no perspective here as the road forks, glides at an angle into a small wood to bring about a break before delivering to disconcerted eyes the villa "full frame" in its meadow, with its radical geometry, perched volumes, and dazzling whiteness.

At this precise moment begins a track-in during which the façade gradually invades the frame until it forms a close-up, then gives way to a close-up of the east ground-floor wall, while the car moves straight ahead before turning into a relatively tight bend.

After coming to a stop, chauffeur and visitors remain speechless. Where they would traditionally find themselves in front of imposing glazed doors, protected by richly decorated ironwork and flanked by powerful stone walls, they discover a simple metal door set in a glass wall. Here begins the

Associated.
The automobile is systematically present in the photographs of Le Corbusier's "white villas", such as the Villa Church and the Villa Stein-de-Monzie (Fondation Le Corbusier, Paris).

Simple.
Garments cling to the body and heels rise to make up the outfits of the visitors who move up the ramps of the villa (Galliera, Musée de la Mode, Paris).

discovery of a new universe that the automobile greatly helped stage by inducing a continuous movement that the body would then extend.

The disintegration of social codes

The terrestrial expression of Le Corbusier's fascination for ocean liners, the automobile embodied the new spirit that animated the new man, born in Eastern Europe in 1917 and who quickly spread through Scandinavia and Germany and whose architecture endeavoured to define the city and housing, necessarily new.

"Architecture suffocates in routine," declared Le Corbusier. New practices freed it, as affirmed by the Villa Savoye, the "five points"—the pilotis, the roof-garden, the open plan, the free façade, and the strip window—constituting the implements that enabled it to succeed and not an end in themselves. From this point of view, the house seems to be a real machine for deconstructing social codes, for shaking up the spatial organisations expressing them and the slightest decorum enhancing them. To do so, it systematically destabilises the usual sensations, the gaze no longer encountering the signs enabling it to identify a town house or country house.

No more perron flanked by a few columns: a single door opens directly onto a hall on the same level.

No more imposing entrance hall with its perfect symmetry, dark atmosphere, decorum, and marble floors: the dissymmetric hall is bathed in natural light because it is open to the outside, slips between the columns, gives a glimpse of a washbasin, a corridor, and a ramp.

No more servants' stairs hidden in the depths of the building as an element of the invisible movement of the servants. Even worse, this staircase looks like a sculpture, like that of Charles de Beistegui's flat on the Champs-Élysées or that of Le Corbusier in his own home in Rue Nungesser-et-Coli.

No more thick freestone walls, symbols of power and stability: the walls are thin and smooth, sometimes glazed, and the concrete of the posts is untreated. This spareness even leads to discreet allusions to the windows and spiral stairs of the industrial world.

No more staircases with ironwork festoons that claimed to highlight the grace of bodies in motion, the elegance of the clothes they wore: the white of the walls, the "industrial" floor, and the ramp are in tune with fitted dresses, fine-leather shoes, and the bright colours of fine fabrics.

No more main staircase, the showpiece of classical architects: two straight lines, articulated by means of a small landing, inch along an exterior terrace and lead the visitor without ceremony to the main space of the villa.

No more slow movement at a measured pace, the gaze scrutinizing social rank, the swaying of the fabric of heavy, stiff outfits: the slope, covered with over 200 kilograms of rubber 5 millimetres thick, invites an athletic, relaxed gait whether going up or down.

No more protocol embodied by the triumvirate of drawing room, morning room, and dining room: one enters directly through the dining room and crosses it to reach the living room; no partition separates them. And the kitchen itself is not placed in the depths of the house but makes its presence felt behind a single door.

No more mirrors, gilding, genre scenes, tapestries, wall hangings, chandeliers, or richly decorated furniture affirming the hereditary fortune or the quick success in industry or finance: the walls of the social heart of the villa are bare, the cupboards display their aluminium doors, the ceramic of the floor resonates, the light falls from long industrial lighting, the minuscule fireplace protrudes into the room, the windows are horizontal when they have not replaced masonry to make up an entire wall, a sliding section of glass.

No more chiaroscuro created by the combination of windows and centre lights, light sources amplified by the play of mirrors arranged on the walls: daylight penetrates the space that it illuminates through three of the four sides, sculpting pieces of furniture and bodies, capturing the colours of the setting sun the better to cover the walls with them.

No more dark, steamy, and smoky kitchen: the extensive white ceramic surfaces catch the daylight the better to make the space, with its tiled work surfaces and cupboards with metal doors, resemble the new laboratories and hospital rooms. And—a new development—the kitchen is no longer hidden but offers a panoramic view of the landscape of the Seine valley, the house's owners and their servants were thus equal in terms of floor, light, view, and modernity of space and materials.

No more hiding of the structure of the building under intricate decorations. The only spaces where load-bearing structures were observed were the large public buildings and their colonnades or factories with their wooden, metal, or reinforced-concrete frames. Displaying in this way the posts and beams from the vestibule to the terrace, from the bedrooms to the living room—that is, in all the spaces of a domestic interior—affirms a freedom that goes beyond architecture.

The winds of freedom

The bedrooms are also stripped down, their elaborate decorations replaced by bare walls, their heavy curtains by light screens, the heavy wardrobes standing against the walls by shoulder-height cupboards that subdivide the space, creating a boudoir, isolating a toilet area, setting up a spatial transition between corridor and bedroom without, however, recreating an entrance or protecting a reading area.

Up to the doorways of the bedrooms, the space is open: where there once were doors marking thresholds and transitions, the traffic now moves freely, continuously, permeably. As a counterpoint to the parallelepiped containing the main rooms, corridors, landings, ramp, and staircase continuously form and reform a space that may be covered in all directions: vertical, horizontal, oblique.

An even more radical freedom is proposed between the parents' bedroom and bathroom. The Orient moves into the heart of the exterior figure of the Athenian acropolis, inviting bodies to expose themselves, to express the solitary or shared pleasure of the bath, to give themselves up to a sensual lasciviousness prolonging that pleasure. This space single-handed-ly affirms that the rejection of the garments in heavy fabrics that buried bodies was not the result of a fashion in clothing but the sign of a new relationship between bodies, and between bodies and social life. This is also the signification of the photos taken on the beaches of Deauville where, in the 1930s, young women exposed themselves topless to the heat of the sun and to the gaze of men, stretched out on rows of deckchairs. Thus appeared, in an atmosphere not devoid of eroticism, the photo of Charlotte Perriand from the back, naked from the waist up in front of a snowy mountain landscape, taken by Pierre Jeanneret, or that of Le Corbusier painting in the nude on the terrace of his cabin in Roquebrune-Cap-Martin.

There is, moreover, an almost sensual gentleness in the gestures made throughout the villa: the feet glide over the rubber ramp, the hand brushes against the concrete handrail, a slight

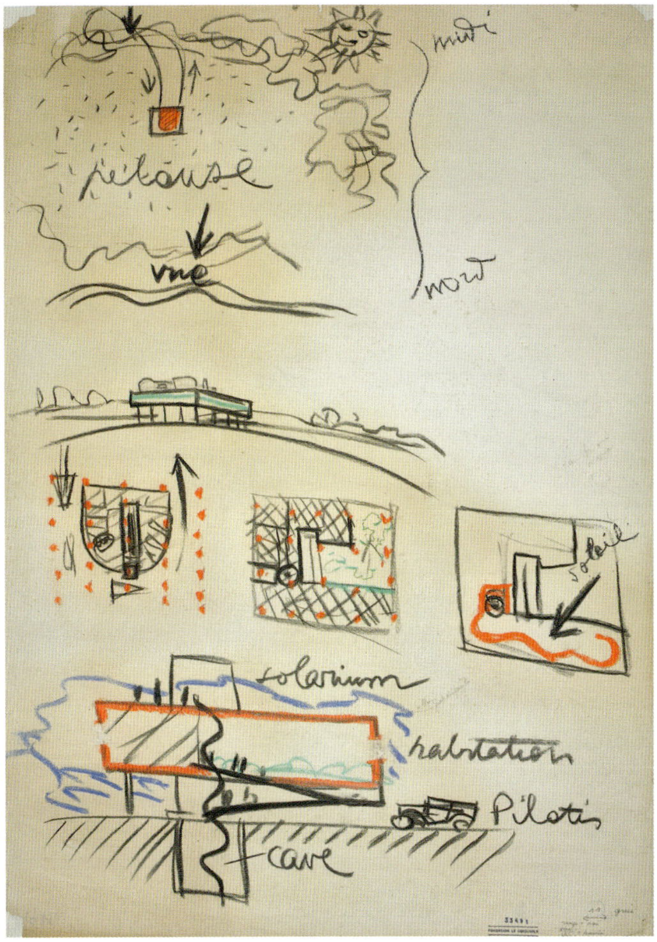

Explained.
In a few freehand sketches, during the fifth of the ten lectures given in Buenos Aires on 11 October 1929, Le Corbusier summed up the design of the villa in relation to the characteristics of the site, the shape of the plot, the circulation of the automobiles under the pilotis, and the distribution of the main functions (Fondation Le Corbusier, Paris, 33.491).

Drawn.
Between the initial idea and the definitive plans, the villa lost a floor and an exterior staircase, but gained in compactness and simplicity.

Top: Perspective sketch, Indian ink, lead pencil, vellum tracing paper.
Bottom: Perspective of the villa, plot, and vegetation, Indian ink, lead pencil and crayon, vellum tracing paper (Fondation Le Corbusier, Paris, 19.423 and 31.522).

gesture slides open or shut the cupboard door, the large glass wall, one of the many horizontal windows, the curtains that protect against the sun. And as in the drawing by the architect representing the plan of the bathroom, the body of the woman nestles on the tiled chaise longue, under the man's gaze. The evident nomadism of the objects continues the lightness of the gestures and the bodies in motion: a shelf projects into the living room until it becomes a fireplace, a wardrobe into the room until it forms a partition.

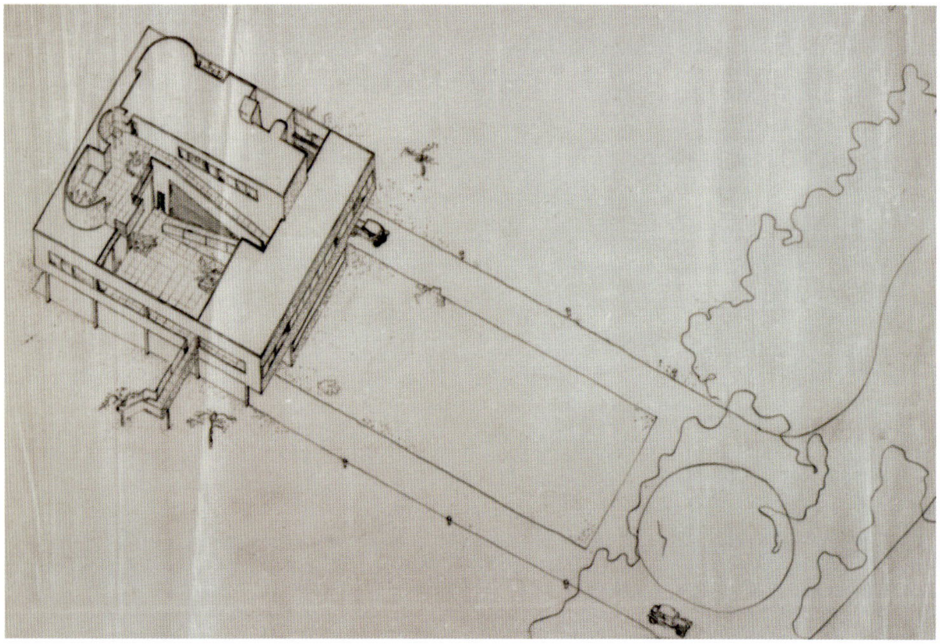

Nature and the body

Unlike other projects by Le Corbusier or Mallet-Stevens, including the athletic Villa Noailles inaugurated in Hyères in December 1925, the solarium of the villa lacks fitness equipment. It nevertheless illustrates the transformation of the relationship of the body to nature through the pleasure of exposing it to the rays of the sun in an attitude that is more Nordic than Mediterranean.

But the terrace also demonstrates the new relationship that man has forged with nature. The belvedere facing the interior garden of the house, except for a window framing the Seine valley, focuses attention on the modern man's break with the natural soil, a break that culminated in the design of the Cités Radieuses of Marseille, Rezé, Firminy, and Briey in France, and that of Berlin in Germany. The fertile soil becomes an object of contemplation from a mineral platform punctuated with a few planters. The villa is not immersed in nature but renounces it; the city dweller breaks with his rural roots and establishes a relationship with nature considered solely in relation to natural elements and landscapes. This distancing was signalled by the construction of a series of windows opening onto the west façade of the terrace, a strategy already adopted by Mallet-Stevens for the Villa Noailles in Hyères.

The avant-garde and modernity

Was the villa provocative? Most certainly not for its owners, who made no remarks about the aesthetics or the functioning of their residence in the many letters sent to the two architects about the technical faults of the villa. The possible reactions of their friends and family members have not survived.

Probably the most surprised was Le Corbusier himself, not by the spaces that he had designed with Pierre Jeanneret but by the layout chosen by his clients. When, in the presentation of the villa that he distributed, he stated that he built it "for clients entirely without preconceptions, new or old", did he mean that they were so open-minded that he was able to guide them in the choices of the layout of the house? Or was he subtly putting distance between himself and the content of the photos of the interior of the villa, published from 1931 and showing furniture totally unlike that he designed with Pierre Jeanneret and Charlotte Perriand?

The villa did not contain a prestigious collection of artworks like that of Raoul La Roche, works by its owner like those of Ozenfant and Lipchitz, or pieces of furniture designed by the architect and his friends. Unlike the Churches, who stayed in international luxury hotels, travelled, took the waters in the fashionable towns of Old Europe, organised unforgettable fireworks in Ville-d'Avray, and had three Bugattis and a Hispano-Suiza, Pierre and Eugénie Savoye seemed to lead a simple life. The villa was not their main residence, they furnished it with pieces that were either antique or that expressed the moderate taste of the designers affiliated to the Société des Artistes Décorateurs. The avant-gardist spirit of the designers of the Union des Artistes Modernes did not seem to hold their attention. The villa thus typifies the duality of the 1920s conception of modernity: radical in its architecture, which reflects the designs most at odds with the previous era, and temperate in its interior layout, which favoured elements moderately modernising the classic lines.

This dichotomy perhaps justifies the haste with which Le Corbusier had the villa—still empty of all furniture—published in two journals, one whose complete support he had, *L'Architecture d'aujourd'hui* (no. 2, 1930), the other more institutional, *L'Architecte* (no. 9, September 1930). It accounts for the difficulties as soon as there is the temptation to refurnish the villa. Should its original fitting out be illustrated by refurnishing it with the equivalent of the pieces chosen by the couple? Or should the spirit of Le Corbusier in partnership with Pierre Jeanneret and Charlotte Perriand be demonstrated by using the chairs, armchairs, stools, chests, and tables designed by the trio? Or should the villa be left empty as has been done up to now to emphasise the spatial and building work of the two architects at the risk of further eclipsing those behind this achievement, their clients?

From left to right: Plans of the ground floor, of the first and second floors, lead pencil, Indian ink, tracing paper study. Drawings of 17 December 1928 (Fondation Le Corbusier, Paris, 19.431 and 19.432).

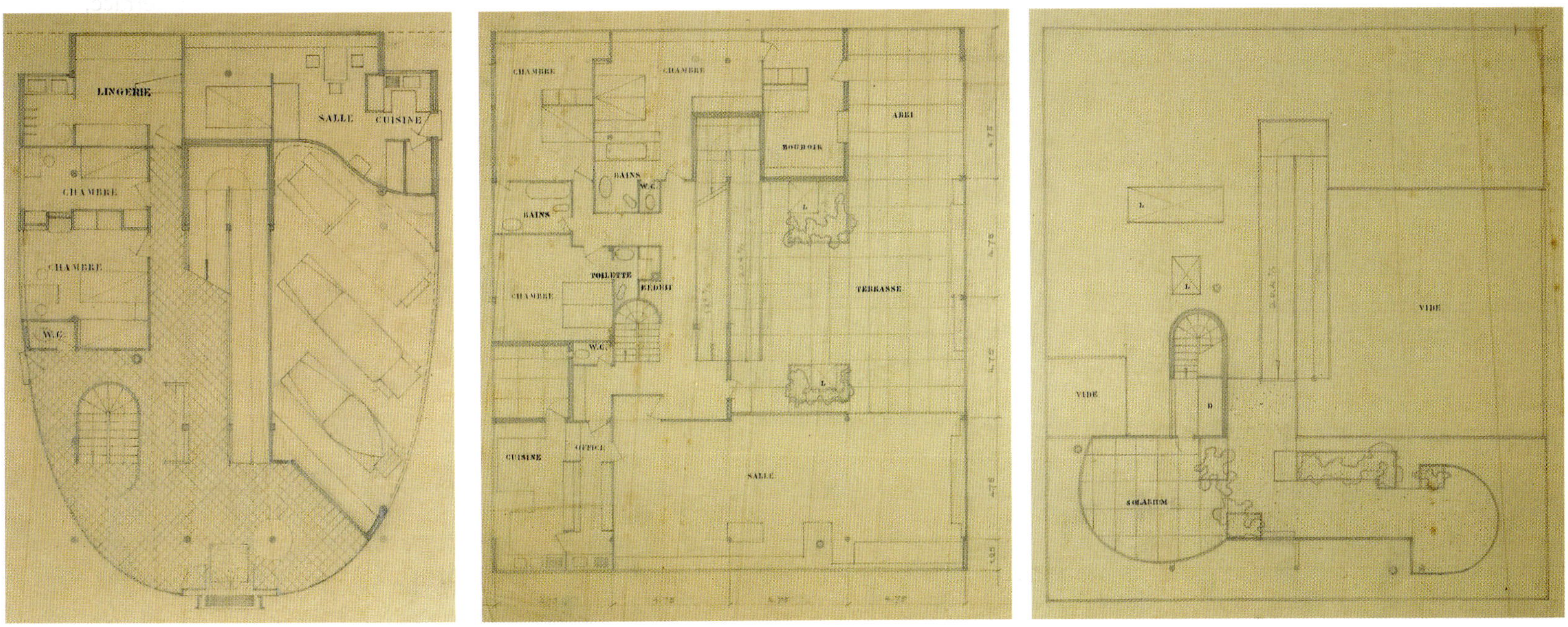

From anger to abandonment

The design process—more than the building work—took its toll on the relationship between the architects and the Savoyes. The allocated budget only appeared to be respected because the architects systematically took as a basis the lowest tenders they received and did not include the warden's lodge in their figures. The cost was also increased by the changes made during construction, including the prefabricated elements. The villa ended up costing twice the agreed price. The economic crisis of 1929 produced a backdrop that must have temporarily weighed heavy on the business and prosperity of Pierre Savoye and accentuated the inconvenience of such overspending.

That is probably why the defects noted and the discomfort felt were a painful experience for the couple. "It is raining in my house," lamented Eugénie Savoye in a letter sent to Le Corbusier and Pierre Jeanneret on 7 September 1936. "We are shivering," raged Pierre Savoye who complained about the inability of the boiler and the radiators to maintain a suitable temperature. "We are bathing in humidity," the couple complained, even more attentive to this fact as their son Roger suffered from tuberculosis.

Himself subject to the estoppel of the firm that took over from Cormier, Le Corbusier remained silent, minimised, or equivocated, thus increasing his clients' disquiet. He incurred the criticism contained in a letter sent to him by Pierre Savoye on 7 September 1937: "There always seems to be someone in your office to send me visitors, but not to reply to my letters." As firms were late in intervening and surveys were late in arriving, Pierre Savoye asked for the plans in order to intervene himself and threatened to take the architects to court. To avoid the procedure, on 31 October 1937, Le Corbusier sent him a vigorous epistolary plea in which he stated: "You should think of us as the friends of your house."

The villa threatened by the automobile industry

As Pierre Savoye had sensed, war broke out. Anxious to avoid the consequences of any future bombing of the capital, he left Paris for the villa: the couple, their son, and their servants lived there until they went to Brive. But after the war, only Eugénie and Roger returned to the villa damaged by the successive occupying forces and picked the fruit of its orchard.

Paradoxically, it was the automobile industry that in part sealed the fate of the villa. In 1937 American carmaker Ford chose the Seine valley, and more precisely Poissy, to set up a 50,000-square-metre factory on a 25-hectare site. Opened in 1939, the factory was requisitioned by the Germans then taken over after the war by Simca, a French carmaker well-known at that time for its popular models. As the factory expanded rapidly, accommodation was built for the workers. The authorities chose the vast agricultural plateau in front of the entrance to the villa to construct buildings to house thousands of people. Built by the architect Charles-Gustave Stoskopf, this complex consisted of the local shopping centre, medical facilities, church, and schools essential to community life. The only thing that was missing was a secondary school, which the Ministry of Education, together with the elected representatives of Poissy, chose to build on the site of the Villa Savoye, which meant that the villa had to be demolished.

There were two simultaneous reactions. The first was that of Eugénie Savoye and her son Roger, who wanted to obtain a fair financial compensation for the expropriated property although Eugénie was not in favour of the alienation of the property. Roger mentioned the profound emotional ties that prompted his mother to enjoy the peaceful use of the place for as long as she lived. The second was led by Le Corbusier to save his landmark work.

Yes to apples, no to the villa

Eugénie Savoye, a widow since 1950, and her son, then aged fifty, did not oppose the principle of the expropriation. They reckoned that the villa had not brought them enough pleasure during the ten years that they lived there for them to devote large sums to making it habitable a second time.

But while the banks of the Seine were allotted to the automobile, chemicals, and energy industries, the hills bordering the river were covered with orchards. This local characteristic, within the context of the expropriation procedure, resulted in the value of the property (27,635,000 francs) being determined in relation to that of the apples produced by the fruit trees that the Savoyes had planted on 3 of the 7 hectares surrounding the villa.

Such a calculation demonstrates that architectural masterpieces did not exist for either the French government in charge of the transmission of culture and knowledge, or the elected representatives of the municipality of Poissy.

Eugénie and Roger did not accept the proposition, which did not take into account the value of the villa (20 million francs) or that of the plot (105 million francs). Several legal proceedings took place until, in late 1959, the court set compensation that was acceptable by both the City of Poissy and the Savoyes (1,271,875 new francs). Legally, the villa could then be demolished and the secondary school built by the architect Jacques Chauliat.

Le Corbusier bombards Malraux

However, in the meantime, the resistance was organised because Eugénie and Roger Savoye warned Le Corbusier of the threats hanging over the villa. The architect immediately mobilised his friends and acquaintances, and activated his networks. In France, the Cercle d'Études Architecturales chaired by Pierre Sonrel interceded with André Malraux. Simultaneously, a committee to safeguard the villa formed around Henri Quillé, a young town planner who brought together the close relations of the architect, including Roger and Édith Aujame, Vladimir Bodiansky, and Charlotte Perriand, as well as young professionals such as Jean Renaudie, Jean-Louis Véret, Gérard Thurnauer, and Pierre Riboulet, the future founders of the Atelier de Montrouge. The most vehement protests came from the United States, South America, and Northern Europe, at the instigation of the renowned historian Sigfried Giedion and the architect Josep Lluís Sert. Personalities, institutions, and professionals tirelessly sent letters and telegrams to the office of André Malraux. The sudden interest annoyed the minister, who accused the architect of being the instigator of the "spontaneous" wave of protests. Le Corbusier slyly asserted that he had kept out of all the agitation: "The Savoye affair broke out totally and completely without my knowledge," he confirmed on 11 March 1960.

While his action did allow the villa to be saved, nothing went as the architect had planned.

Hopes and failures

There were insufficient funds to save the villa. A specific project was needed; Le Corbusier hastened to find one: a Le Corbusier museum initiated by a Le Corbusier foundation. In the letter that he sent to Sigfried Giedion on 11 March 1959, he set out the considerable assets of this structure: "Thousands of drawings, perhaps 200 paintings, the entire collection of architectural and town plans, copyrights to some fifty books, my flat in the Rue Nungesser-et-Coli, and the small Maison du Lac." But the foundation was later set up in the house in the Square du Docteur-Blanche in the sixteenth arrondissement of Paris donated by Raoul La Roche.

He simultaneously endeavoured to get the construction of the secondary school cancelled: "The charm of this property it that it stands in the midst of grass, in the middle of nowhere. Solitude and silence are the main reasons why it is so pleasant," he reminded André Malraux in a letter of 8 June 1959. He was simply asked to ratify the plans of the architect of the secondary school and to ratify the reduction of the plot attached to the villa from 7 hectares to 1 hectare, only obtaining the moving of the gymnasium to preserve part of the view of the Seine valley.

"There is no question of another architect being put in charge of the work," Le Corbusier raged in a letter to one of André Malraux's colleagues on 5 March 1960 after a meeting about the future of the villa held on 18 February. Paradoxically, a listing procedure deprived the architect of any possibility of restoring his own building as the job was entrusted to Jean Dubuisson to whom he finally handed over the twenty-eight original plans.

Respected.
The strength of the relationships established between the roof garden, the main living area, the exterior ramp, and the solarium endure, from the first sketch to the finished building (Fondation Le Corbusier, Paris, 19.425 for the sketch and L2-17-173 for the photo of the building under construction. Photograph of the delivered building published in *L'Architecte* 9 [September 1930]).

Monitored.
Year after year, the progression of the work on the main space of the villa was illustrated in photographs: under construction in 1929 (*L'Architecture vivante*, summer 1931), bare in 1930 (*L'Architecture d'aujourd'hui*, 1930), and furnished in 1931 (*L'Architecture vivante*, summer 1931).

Refined.
With a few simple props, the photographer of the journal *L'Architecture vivante* (summer 1931) managed to convey the chic atmosphere of the villa and suggest what everyday life there was like.

In 1959 Le Corbusier was impatient for the work to begin. In 1960 he put the office in battle order to prepare for the restoration work and consulted contractors. In 1961 he wanted to take possession of the keys. In 1962 he intended to launch the renovation work on 15 July. In December 1963, he asked Dubuisson: "What do we do with the Villa Savoye?" On 15 May 1965, he lost patience with Dubuisson's slowness, writing to him: "Do me a favour and finish the Villa Savoye that you are in charge of restoring." On 3 June 1965, he wrote to André Malraux: "At the fateful hour, the Villa Savoye, historical monument, will collapse from waiting too long."
He died two months later. The villa was listed seven months later and opened to the public twenty-two years later.

A radiant delight

"The house is an object that interests both the animal and the cerebral in us because inside it we are subjected to its constraints. And it is for this reason that the problem of housing today fascinates a new society that eagerly seeks new rules capable of counterbalancing the new tension that drives it," declared Le Corbusier in his book *Une maison. Un palais* (Paris: Crès et Cie, 1928). This tension no doubt still exists in the villa, which has maintained intact its power to delight and charm all those who, whatever their culture or country of origin, explore its volumes, linger in the double living room, isolate themselves in the boudoir of the couple's bedroom, marvel at their bathroom, let their bodies turn in the spiral of the staircase or the ramp. Their radiant faces express emotions that are changing, unsettling, and always rewarding.

A CLOSER LOOK

Bright.
Seen from its north access, the villa gives an impression of quiet strength even though it appears to be standing on a flat site. The pilotis and the visual fissure created by the horizontal windows immediately provide a key to understanding its architecture: the void fully participates in the design of the habitable volume.

Following page:

Meaningful.
Determined by the turning circle of automobiles, the curve of the glass wall is punctuated with vertical metal sashes. This geometric treatment evokes the two extremes of movement: split up into its component gestures on photographic film by Jules Marey, accelerated by the speed that brought closer to the trees lining the roads as seen in the cinema of the 1930s.

Different.
Columns in the middle of the hall, a staircase coiled up on itself, and a ramp to get to the upper floor: many of the couple's guests were no doubt disconcerted by their first contact with the interior volumes of the villa. Did they perceive the symmetry of the glass wall and the pillars of the entrance discreetly evoking a bygone order?

Following page:

Complex.
In its upper section and through the filter of the metal stiles striating the plate glass windows, the incline reveals the roof garden, the living room, and the play of light and shade that animates the white walls and the structural elements painted in the same colour.

Open.
A simple landing and a thin door precede the single volume that was the setting or both meals and shared moments. This volume, through the glass wall comprising its south façade and the windows running along its two other façades, is reminiscent of the primitive shelter. According to the season and the time of day, the reflections even dematerialise its ceiling.

Following page:

Unobtrusive.
The glass wall gives a panoramic view of the roof garden. Like a CinemaScope camera, it frames a complex geometry featuring the running void of the exterior window, the shelter comprising the south façade, the overhang of the boudoir of the parents' bedroom, and the oblique lines of the ramp leading to the solarium.

Studied.
Responding to the glazed door giving access to the single volume is the door separating the dining room from the kitchen, rendered invisible by a simple cupboard. The cupboards, equipped with aluminium sliding doors like all the cupboards in the house, are accessible from the kitchen and the pantry.

Landscaped.
Running water, washtubs, large work surfaces, white ceramic tiles, and electrical appliances: the kitchen is functional, modern, and hygienic. The large windows, which open, provide the people working there with the added charm of the view over the Seine valley and natural ventilation.

Colourful.
Visible from the first-floor landing, at the end of a straight corridor, the son's bedroom is open to the east and the south. The simple room is enriched by the use of colour, the curve of the wall whose shape echoes that of bathtub in the bathroom, and the multipurpose piece of furniture that forms a protected space.

Dramatised.
On the opposite side from the dining room and at the end of a spectacular walk, the parents' bedroom opens onto a series of wall cupboards that make up a dressing room in pastel tones. The wardrobes conceal the bathroom with its overhead natural lighting.

Following page:

Glorified.
The pleasure of water is predominant in terms of surface area and visual impact in the parents' bedroom, the fixed chaise longue between the bedroom and the bathroom has become one of the emblematic images of the villa. It diverts attention from the monumental effect created by the posts into which the bedhead was sunk.

Towards the parents' bedroom

Subtle.
The natural lighting enlivened the walls entirely covered with rectangular white earthenware tiles, giving the relatively narrow volume of the bathroom a remarkable and changing atmosphere. This treatment accentuates the geometric forms of the bathtub and the curves of the chaise longue.

 The bathroom of the parents' bedroom

Interiority.
The parents' bedroom is extended by a boudoir that combines long horizontal windows open to the south, low cupboards, and a flap for reading or writing facing the terrace. The window frames a close view of the roof garden, filtered by the vegetation arranged in a planter.

Multiple.
A simple door separates the boudoir from the shelter at the end of the roof garden.The villa has three passages. The first is the spiral staircase linking the subterranean world to the sky (from the cellar to the solarium). The second is the ramp the gives access to all the interior and exterior spaces from the bottom of the entrance hall to the solarium that crowns the house. The third comprises a more private horizontal path: it serves the first level from the landing, goes through the parents' bedroom, and crosses the roof garden to reach the living room or go back to the landing.

Sensual.
The successive stages of the ramp and the curves of the spiral staircase comprise a suite of subtle and abstract architectural variations against a backdrop of whites accentuated by the black handrails that unfurl or coil up.

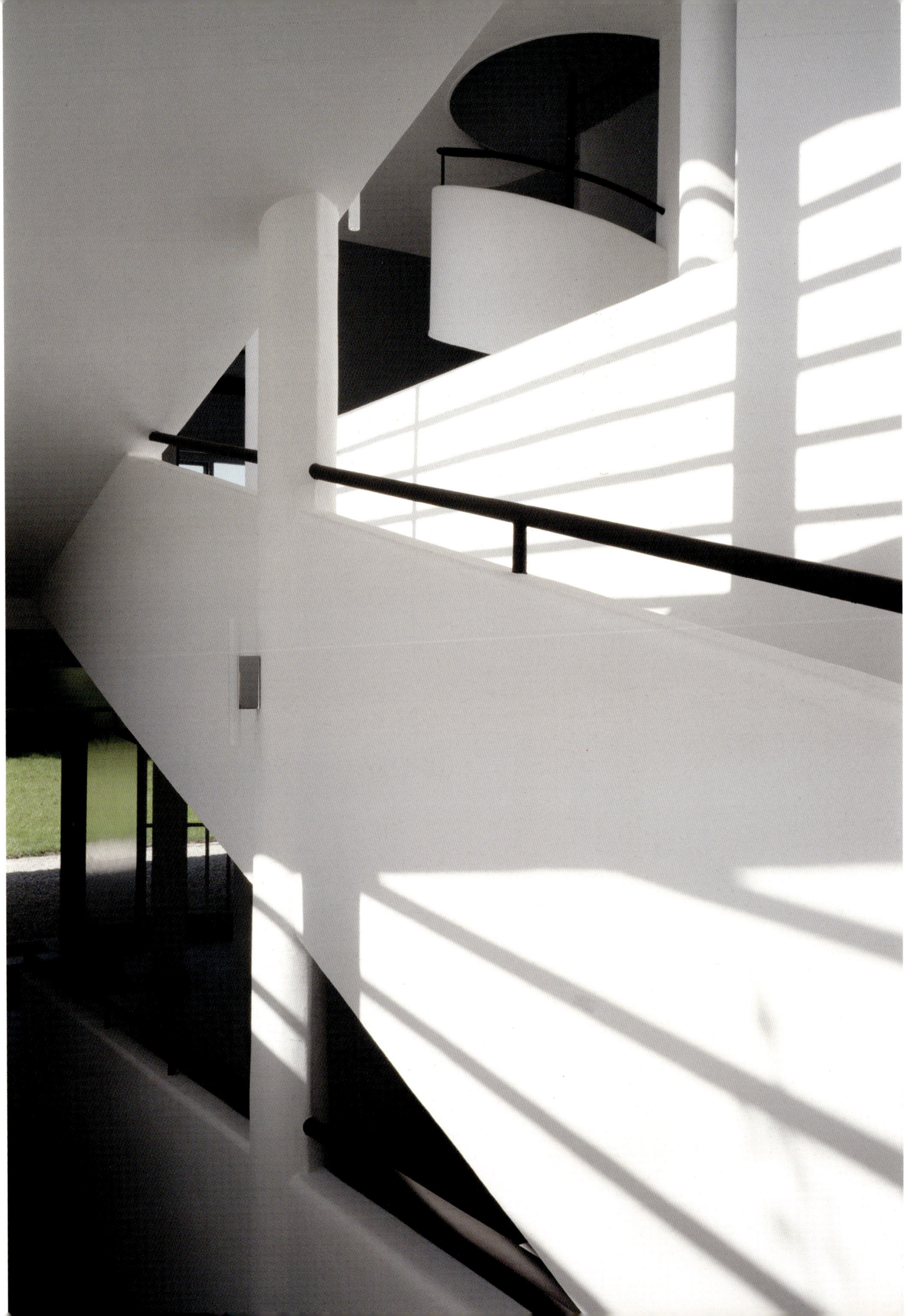

Repeated.
The interior spaces of the villa combine large visual openings: some vertical, crossed by the diagonals of the ramp; some horizontal, formed by the corridors leading to the first-floor bedrooms. In both cases, the staircase provides a discreet or imposing counterpoint.

Exit.
Owners and visitors leave the villa through the glazed door of the entrance hall and reach the automobiles waiting for them underneath the pilotis, the chauffeurs having parked them in the garage integrated into the volume of the ground floor. A runner enables the ground-floor door to slide following the curve of the façade.

Varied.
Although they were designed according to a great visual coherence and feature the same identifiers (horizontal windows and pilotis), the four façades—south and east on the left, north and west on the right—propose subtle variations of solids and voids, transparent and opalescent, and the inscription of the elements of the solarium on the band of the façade.

Following page:

Highlighted.
Artificial lighting fully reveals the transparency of the entrance hall and of the various rooms or spaces of the north façade of the villa. It simultaneously highlights the strength and equilibrium of the masses and the finely studied detail of the rhythms of the various vertical elements.

Revealed.
The villa is no longer isolated on its land as industrial growth and urban sprawl have profoundly altered its surroundings over three-quarters of a century. The broader perspective also allows the projection on the ground of the plan of the villa to be fully visualised, the last sign before the passage in front of the warden's house.

IN DEPTH

The guardian angels of the villa

As soon as the salvage and listing of the villa were considered, the question of its restoration arose. Since the decisions to salvage and list it were made, several architects have undertaken its restoration and upkeep.

Jean Dubuisson

Known in Paris for having taken part in the Maine-Montparnasse urban renewal project in Paris and having designed the Musée des Arts et Traditions Populaires in the Bois de Boulogne, Jean Dubuisson was an *architecte des Bâtiments civils et Palais nationaux.*
As such, he was appointed in 1963 to supervise the first restoration of the villa, which he undertook after a long diagnostic phase and within the context of limited funds, spread over several years. Moreover, from his nomination to the summer of 1965, Dubuisson intervened under the direct or indirect pressure of Le Corbusier, smarting from having been excluded from the project that he deemed only he was able to see through. Dubuisson, an experienced architect, seems to have been ill at ease in this new role, having to deal with the bankruptcy of the firm in charge of the woodwork, which, with the windows, constituted the Achilles heel of his intervention, completed in 1967.

Ivan Gury

With his father-in-law, the architect Jean-Baptiste Hourlier—the man behind the reconstructions of Lorient and Saumur—he designed several schools and council blocks in the Paris region.
It was as *architecte des Bâtiments civils et Palais nationaux* that he succeeded Jean Dubuisson and oversaw the restoration of the villa until 1985, endeavouring to repair the faulty workmanship of the first restoration.

Jean-Louis Véret

After having worked in North Africa alongside Michel Écochard, who declared himself in favour of the construction of the secondary school on the Villa Savoye site, he worked in Ahmedabad, India, from 1953 to 1955 as a collaborator of the Le Corbusier studio.
Having founded the Atelier de Montrouge with Jean Renaudie, Gérard Thurnauer, and Pierre Riboulet, he later set up on his own in 1981. Appointed curator of the villa in March 1985, he extensively researched the history of its construction and the interventions carried out since then, which led him to draw up an "identity card" for the building. He thus prepared for, with the assistance of his colleague Laurence Razy, the second major renovation of the villa.

Bruno Chauffert-Yvart and Laurence Razy

Architecte en chef des Bâtiments de France, head of the architecture and cultural heritage department of the Yvelines, the department in which the Villa Savoye was built, Bruno Chauffert-Yvart took on Laurence Razy to finish the preparations for, from 1992 to 1996, another complete restoration of the villa, whose interior and exterior polychromy they restored. The villa was closed for a year in 1997 to facilitate the works and the creation of a reception area for the public.

Philippe Oudin

Architecte en chef des monuments historiques, he managed the maintenance operations, an assignment made easier by the renovation of 1997, while the villa welcomed a steadily increasing number of visitors, and organised events and exhibitions.

Pascal Prunet

Architecte en chef des monuments historiques, he has been in charge of the upkeep of the villa since 2009.
He restored the warden's house and its original polychromy, and had to deal with the question of restoring the polychromy of the solarium attested to in several period accounts.

"Despite the fact that it looks like a ruin, the villa is impeccable from a construction point of view and could be restored at little cost" (Le Corbusier, letter to André Malraux, 20 May 1960).

A series of buildings

Charles-Édouard Jeanneret, known as Le Corbusier, by Jean and Joël Martel, plaster, 1966 (Villa Savoye, Poissy).

The Maison Louis-Carré by the architect Alvar Aalto, 2 chemin du Saint-Sacrement, Bazoches-sur-Guyonne.

The Villa Savoye is generally presented as the last of a series of homes and artists' studios known as the "white villas". Built by Le Corbusier and Pierre Jeanneret, they bear witness to their innovative spirit and to the architectural avant-garde of the 1920s.

The white villas

Except for the destroyed Villa Church, the other buildings of the series may be seen in Paris and its suburbs.
In chronological order of their design:
– the Villa Besnus (1923), massively altered, 85 boulevard de la République, Vaucresson, Hauts-de-Seine;
– the Ozenfant studio (1923–24), 53 avenue Reille, Paris, 14th arrondissement;
– the Villa La Roche (1923–25 and 1928), 8–10 square du Docteur-Blanche, Paris, 16th arrondissement;
– the Villa Jeanneret-Raaf (1923–25), 8–10, square du Docteur-Blanche, Paris, 16th arrondissement (headquarters of the Fondation Le Corbusier);
– the Lipchitz studio (1924–25), 9 allée des Pins, Boulogne-Billancourt, Hauts-de-Seine;
– the Miestchaninoff studio (1924–25), 7 rue des Arts, Boulogne-Billancourt;
– the Villa Ternisien (1925–26), 5 rue Denfert Rochereau / allée des Pins, Boulogne-Billancourt;
– the Villa Planeix (1925–28), 24 *bis* boulevard Masséna, Paris, 13th arrondissement;
– the Villa Cook (1926–29), 6 rue Denfert-Rochereau, Boulogne-Billancourt;
– the Villa Stein-de-Monzie, known as "Les Terrasses" (1926–28), 17 rue du Professeur-Victor-Pauchet, Vaucresson.

The 1930s spirit in Paris

In the 14th arrondissement of Paris, the Ozenfant studio was near several interesting buildings, including the Cité Internationale Universitaire (the Swiss and Brazilian pavilions were designed by Le Corbusier). Also worth seeing: the studio of Georges Braque designed by Auguste Perret, 6 rue Georges-Braque; the Villa Guggenbuhl designed by André Lurçat, 14 rue Nansouty; and the studios designed by Auguste Perret and André Lurçat on both sides of a private road, Villa Seurat, in the 14th arrondissement.

The 1930s in Boulogne-Billancourt

Not far from the building at 24 rue Nungesser-et-Coli (open on Saturday from 10 a.m. to 1 p.m. and from 1.30 p.m. to 5 p.m.), a presentation of three "white villas" located in Boulogne-Billancourt is part of the avant-garde architecture walking tour organised by the Musée des Années 30 (Espace Landowski, 28 avenue André-Morizet).
This tour also features works by Auguste Perret, Robert Mallet-Stevens, and André Lurçat. The museum is next to the town hall designed by Tony Garnier (see the interior).

Near the Villa Savoye

In Poissy, the town hall and the theatre are housed in a single edifice, built in 1937, which illustrated the will to facilitate access to culture. Built by the architects Pierre Mathé and Henri Calsat, it contains works of art such as a pediment by the sculptor Ossip Zadkine (complete visit during the Journées du Patrimoine heritage days).
In Mézy-sur-Seine (route d'Apremont) is the villa of Paul Poiret, known as "Le Château", designed by Robert Mallet-Stevens. It was not only the famous fashion designer's home, but also a place where he could present his creations. It is imposing, forming, on the hill overlooking the Seine, a white mass visible from the A 13 motorway (a private property that is open during the Journées du Patrimoine heritage days).
A little further afield, in Bazoches-sur-Guyonne, and more recent (1960), is the only villa designed in France by the Finnish architect Alvar Aalto for the gallery owner Louis Carré (www.maisonlouiscarre.fr).

1

2

3

4

5

1. Ozenfant studio, 53 avenue Reille, Paris, 14th arrondissement.

2. Villa Cook, 6 rue Denfert-Rochereau, Boulogne-Billancourt.

3. Lipchitz studio, 9 allée des Pins, Boulogne-Billancourt.

4. The villas La Roche and Jeanneret-Raaf, 8–10 square du Docteur-Blanche, Paris, 16th arrondissement.

5. Villa Stein-de-Monzie, 17 rue du Professeur-Victor-Pauchet, Vaucresson.

Centre des monuments nationaux

President
Isabelle Lemesle

Managing director
Fabrice Benkimoun

Publishing director
Jocelyn Bouraly

Publications coordinator
Clair Morizet

Assistant publications coordinator
Karin Franques

Editorial and documentation coordinator
Anne-Sophie Grouhel – Le Tellec

Translator
Chrisoula Petridis

Graphic design
Cyril Cohen
Régis Dutreuil

Layout
Miyo Edit - Christophe Petit

Production coordinator
Carine Merse

Photoengraving
Jouve Orléans, Saran

Printing
IME, Baume-les-Dames, France

Dépôt légal: June 2011
ISBN: 978-2-7577-0140-9

Acknowledgements

The author and the Éditions du patrimoine would like to extend their warm thanks to everyone at the Villa Savoye for their kind interest in this project.

Photographic credits

Akg-images/Archives CDA/Saint-Genès: 62b
All rights reserved: 2
CMN/Jean-Christophe Ballot: front cover, 20, 22-23, 24, 25, 26-27, 30-31, 39, 42, 43, 45, 50, 54, 55, 56-57, 59
CMN/Philippe Berthé: 62t
CMN/11h45: 21, 28, 29, 32, 33, 34, 35, 36, 37, 38, 40-41, 44, 46, 47, 48, 49, 51, 52, 53, 58
Fondation Le Corbusier/ADAGP: 4, 5, 7t, 9tl and tr, 11, 12, 13, 16, 17, 18
Fondation Le Corbusier/ADAGP/Olivier Martin-Gambier: 63
Galliera/Roger-Viollet: 9b
Victor Gubbins: 61

Front cover
The spiral staircase.